DEBBIE BILEK

I Wanted to be a Boy

Finding Truth in Your Gender Identity

Dedicated to the Next Generation
From one Mama Bear who will never stop fighting for
your freedom from the schemes of the enemy.

Contents

Introduction

If you're holding this book, it's likely because you or someone you deeply care about is walking a road filled with questions, emotions, and uncertainty—perhaps even pain. Maybe you're struggling with your own identity, or maybe you're a parent, sibling, or friend of someone who is. Wherever you find yourself, know this: you are not alone.

This book was born from a heart of compassion and a desire to bring peace, clarity, and lasting hope to those navigating the deeply personal journey of gender identity, gender dysphoria, and the broader LGBTQ+ experience. Whether you feel confused, afraid, angry, weary, or are simply searching for answers—this book is for you.

In these pages, you will find a fresh perspective—one that speaks truth with love, grace with conviction, and compassion without compromise. It offers an honest look at the struggles you may be facing and the questions that have weighed heavy on your heart. More importantly, it offers the possibility of rest. Rest from the confusion. Rest from the fear of being misunderstood or rejected. Rest from feeling like you're walking this path in isolation.

For those who have felt silenced, unseen, or unsure of where to turn, this book is an invitation into deeper understanding, healing, and hope. For family members and loved ones, it offers insight, tools for connection, and encouragement to walk in love while holding onto truth.

My hope is that as you read, your heart will begin to settle. That light will begin to shine in the dark places. That you will discover the peace that comes not from having all the answers, but from knowing you are known, seen, and deeply loved by the One who created you.

Let this journey be one of revelation, not rejection. Of restoration, not regret. You were never meant to carry this alone—and you don't have to.

With deep compassion and love from someone who understands,

Debbie Bilek

Chapter 1

Born with Desires

Life is a journey full of sorrow and joy, heartache and grief, victories and celebrations, disappointments and surprises. Deep emotions waver across a grand scale of highs and lows with each new day. We are born in purity and innocence, until the world exposes us to its cruel realities. We do not get to choose where we are planted in this world. We land in the family, the country, the culture, and our location without an inkling of a choice.

We are destined from the beginning of time to be the unique creation that only we can be. No one is like us. No one carries our exact genetic makeup. Even identical twins have variations in their preferences and desires. We are born with specific inclinations, certain likes and dislikes. We are who we are, and we become what we become based upon a variety of factors, including—but not limited to—genetics, culture, environment, opportunities, finances, exposure, family, diet, location, and language.

When I was a child, I wanted to be a boy. My deep hidden desire was to be male, but alas, I was born in a girl's body. I was struggling with what is referred to today as gender identity confusion. If someone experiencing gender identity confusion does not receive support, guidance, or a safe space to explore their feelings, the uncertainty can deepen over time. Without validation or understanding, what begins as questioning may evolve into persistent distress, especially if the individual feels pressured to conform to a gender role that doesn't align with their internal sense of self. In such cases, untreated gender identity confusion can progress into gender dysphoria—a more intense and often painful experience of disconnect between one's gender identity and assigned sex at birth. Early support and open conversations can help prevent this distress from escalating.

The National Health Service in the UK states, "Gender dysphoria is a term that describes a sense of unease that a person may have because of a mismatch between their biological sex and their gender identity. This sense of unease or dissatisfaction may be so intense it can lead to depression and anxiety and have a harmful impact on daily life."[1]

During my childhood, not much was known about gender identity confusion. Today there is ample information available, but it is often difficult to navigate between what is accurate truth and what is false ideology.

Biologically, most humans are born male or female based upon their genetic makeup at conception. This is typically determined by whether the father's sperm contributes an X or a Y chromosome, resulting in XX (female) or XY (male) combinations. At birth, individuals are assigned a sex based on anatomy. When I was a child, ultrasounds were not an option and our gender was announced with joy on the day we were born. The doctor would exclaim to all in the birthing room who were waiting with anticipation: "It's a boy!" Or "It's a girl!" And the parents would rejoice!

Now, more often than not, parents find out the gender of their child through blood tests or ultrasounds long before they meet their baby in the delivery room. Gender reveal parties have become extremely popular, and the baby's gender is still celebrated by all.

As time has progressed, current culture has swayed into the belief system that there are more than two genders in the world. It seems that the list is being added to daily, which has caused much confusion in the minds of children, adolescents, and young adults; thus the new terminology and diagnoses of gender identity confusion and gender dysphoria. There are currently 50 - 80+ recognized genders found in numerous university and medical publications, and the list is growing at an alarming rate. My desire for this book is to bring clarity to those individuals and family members who have been entangled in the gender wars and the turmoil that it has caused.

Though I, personally, came into the world in a girl's body, I "identified" more with my brothers and other males. I thrived playing sports, climbing trees, building forts, wrestling, playing with cars and trucks, army men, and enjoying all of the activities that my brothers enjoyed as the male species.

My parents and other adults gave me dolls which would lay on the floor untouched and unloved. I was enrolled in dance classes where I always felt awkward and uncoordinated. I thrived on the basketball court, on the streets playing baseball and football, and anywhere else I could run, swim, hike, and roam carefree.

I remember desperately wishing that I had been born a boy. I was angry that my brothers got to be boys and that I was stuck in a girl's body. I did most everything they did, but I was still a girl. It seemed life was easier for them. I was much more comfortable in jeans and t-shirts than in dresses, bows, lace, and all things pink, which was the usual attire for girls in my era. I preferred hanging out at the gym in my sweats rather than at the beauty parlor or nail salon. I did not enjoy the girl talk and the drama that often came with being born into the female gender. Boys seemed immune to the extreme emotions that I carried, and I quickly learned to hide and stuff them deep inside.

If you or someone you love is navigating questions of gender identity or experiencing gender dysphoria, this book offers insight, clarity, and compassion. You are not alone. I understand the depth of what you may be feeling, because I've walked this path myself. My aim is to share truth and encouragement that can bring clarity to confusion and peace to inner conflict— guiding you toward your own unique identity and purpose. You are not broken or abnormal. You are deeply valued, profoundly loved, and intentionally created. There is hope, and there is a way forward.

Chapter 2

What is Gender Dysphoria?

According to top ranking Mount Sinai Hospital in New York City, "'Gender dysphoria is the term for a deep sense of unease and distress that may occur when your biological sex does not match your gender identity. In the past, this was called gender identity disorder. For example, you may be assigned at birth as a female gender, but you feel a deep inner sense of being male."[2]

CNN news reported a study that showed the number of gender-affirming surgeries done in the United States nearly tripled between 2016 and 2019, and the rates are climbing with each new year.[3] A study by the National Library of Medicine found that there was a five fold increase in procedures from 2016 - 2021.[4] An article by Reuters in October of 2022 states: "While the number of gender clinics treating children in the United States has grown from zero to more than 100 in the past 15 years – and waiting lists are long – strong evidence of the efficacy and possible long-term consequences of that treatment remains scant."[5] Data from LexisNexis Risk Solutions indicated a 133% rise in insurance claims for gender identity care among individuals under 18 in the U.S. between 2019 and 2023.[6]

At the writing of this book, over 5,700 minors are currently on waiting lists for gender clinic appointments in the UK, with some waiting nearly two years. The youngest patient on the list is under five years old.[7]

Gender dysphoria has quickly become a national epidemic in the United States of America and is on the rise in the UK and other parts of the world as well. Children as young as preschool age are being encouraged to dress as the opposite sex from their sex of origin. Elementary school students are invited to attend clubs that focus on sexual identity. They are taught to use their preferred pronouns and are assisted in choosing new names. In some states, junior high and high school students are permitted to leave school, with the assistance of a school official, to receive gender treatment without parental knowledge or permission.

Never before has society seen such an emphasis on gender and sexual identity over self esteem and education. No wonder there is confusion all around! It's no surprise that depression, anxiety, and suicide rates are on the rise. Children were not meant to handle these adult topics when their brains are still developing. Children and youth are meant to be playing, laughing, learning about nature, science, math, literature, and the amazing world God has made for us to enjoy and thrive in.

As both a mother and a grandmother, I apologize to you, the children, the teenagers, and the young adults whom we have failed. I am sorry that we have not protected you from these sexual agendas that have been pushed to the forefront of society. I cannot undo or fix any of this; but I do know that your childhood dreams, desires, and identity can be restored. You can have a healthy, fulfilling life, no matter how far gone you may feel or what stage you are at in the transitioning process.

Your identity involves so much more than simply your genetic makeup. You were born into a certain bloodline. You were born into a specific race, often a mixed race. Many were born into the religion or the spiritual beliefs of your parents and ancestors. "Identity" refers to your sense of who you are as an individual and as a member of certain social groups. It also refers to your sense of how others may perceive and label you. Your identity doesn't revolve around your sex or your gender. Your identity involves so... much... more.

Wikipedia states, "Identity is the set of qualities, beliefs, personality traits, appearance, and/or expressions that characterize a person or a group. Identity emerges during childhood as children start to comprehend their self-concept and it remains a consistent aspect throughout different stages of life. Identity is shaped by social and cultural factors and how others perceive and acknowledge one's characteristics. The etymology of the term 'identity' from the Latin noun *identitas* emphasizes an individual's mental image of themselves and their 'sameness with others'. Identity encompasses various aspects such as occupational, religious, national, ethnic or racial, gender, educational, generational, and political identities, among others."[8]

There are many definitions of identity, but what matters most is that you have a healthy sense of personal identity, and are able to love and appreciate the unique creation that you are. Your identity extends far beyond your biological sex. It is time to celebrate all of the extraordinary characteristics and traits you are wired with. Your future is bright! You may have questions about who you are, but as you continue to read, more clarity is coming.

In previous generations, masculinity and femininity were viewed in rigid, clearly defined terms. Boys were expected to act like miniature men, with little tolerance for emotional expression or vulnerability. Girls, on the other hand, were encouraged to embrace traditionally delicate traits—adoring all things flowery, frilly, and lacey—while being gentle, reserved, and soft in their demeanor.

This current generation has taken it to the opposite extreme. Individuals who don't fit into those traditional stereotypical gender expectations have deemed themselves "gender fluid", meaning that their gender changes from day to day based upon how they feel at any given moment. This is not realistic and is really messing with the mental health and identity of our young people.

If you were born a female, it is totally possible to embrace the more masculine qualities given to you, but still remain a strong, beautiful female. Many of these women grow up to be powerful leaders in their field of influence. Babies who are born male, but have nurturing, feminine qualities grow up to be the most loving, sensitive and compassionate fathers. They are some of the strongest men I know because they are not afraid to show their true emotions.

It's time to embrace all of your unique qualities and characteristics that make you who you were created to be. You are the only one of you, and nobody can change that! You don't need to strive to be anybody else. Let's celebrate one another just as we are, and encourage each other to be the best version of ourselves that we can be—without dangerous drugs, traumatizing surgeries, and life altering hormone therapy.

Chapter 3

Who am I?

You may have asked yourself questions like, *Who exactly am I? Why am I here on this earth? Why do I feel like a fish out of water? Why don't I fit in?* These are normal questions that we all ask ourselves from time to time. I spent nearly my whole life feeling this way. When I was a little girl, there were expectations of what a girl did and didn't do. I often felt like I was a mistake because I didn't fit the mold that I was being shoved into by my gender. I was labeled a "tomboy" by all who knew me. That was an acceptable label, at the time, for a girl who felt like and wanted to be a boy.

Many years ago when I was coaching my son's U8 soccer team, there was a boy on the team who was not interested in soccer at all. He much preferred playing with girls and dolls. He had such a sweet, nurturing temperament, and was a joy and a delight to all who knew him. His parents were often embarrassed by his more feminine qualities because they had two other sons who were extremely masculine and preferred rough and rowdy activities. They enrolled him into soccer to hopefully motivate him to somehow become more masculine. This only led to much frustration for both he and his parents. Thankfully, he was loved unconditionally by his family, and they all learned together how to encourage him in his unique individuality to grow up to become a healthy man. This little boy has grown into the most loving, doting husband to his wife, and the kindest, most caring father to his precious children.

How fast times have changed! Now, if you publicly share your desires, even as a three year old child who is barely grasping language skills, you are given permission to change your name, change your gender, and transition into the opposite sex. In some states, school officials are mandated to call you by your preferred gender pronouns without revealing any of this to your parents, the very people who love you the most and have your best interest always at heart.

Looking back to my own childhood, I probably would have liked for my parents to have given me a "boy" name and treated me as a boy. Most of my friends were boys and I loved hanging out with them and my brothers. They were my tribe. I was included as one of them. I was not hindered from playing sports on the streets and belonging to their clubs because of my gender. They accepted me for who I was. As an adult, I am so thankful that my family loved me as I was, and allowed me to explore my masculine characteristics *without* altering my gender and my body in a way that could not be undone.

I know that not all of you have had this same experience. I know that you have been denied opportunities, promotions, and inclusion based upon your sexual and gender identity. Life has not been fair. Life has been cruel to you. I am so sorry for what you have had to endure. I'm sorry for the hatred, the isolation, the fear, and the loneliness you have experienced. I'm sorry for those who have been led and permitted to change your names and your bodies permanently. I'm sorry that you did not have a safe space to explore, live, dream, and grow into the unique individual you were created to be.

I understand the deep disconnect at the very core of your heart, as you feel that you do not truly belong to one group or the other. Many of you cry yourselves to sleep at night. You imagine that there is not a soul in the world who understands your internal conflict. I'm here to tell you that you are not alone!

Today, there are people you can talk to and places you can go for answers, but there are also many dangerous voices out there giving really detrimental information that can be life altering and devastating in the long haul. These are extremely serious issues that require thoughtful and respectful consideration. We all need increased discernment so that we do not get led down a path that leads to destruction, chaos, and turmoil in our lives.

I know I hated to hear this when I was a teenager and young adult, but it is a much documented fact: Scientific research has found that the human brain is not fully developed until we reach the age of 25 - 30 years old.[9] How can a child, a teenager, or a young adult possibly make a serious life changing, dramatic decision about altering their sexual organs before this age? It is not a time to begin mutilating your body parts and taking dangerous hormones, until you have the full capacity

14

to understand the serious consequences you are choosing to engage in.

I share this information in hopes that you will pause before moving forward with something so drastic that you may regret it for the rest of your life. I encourage you to talk with a trusted parent, friend, pastor, counselor, teacher, or loved one. Choose a person who truly knows you and has your absolute best interest at heart.

If you have already moved forward in transitioning, please don't lose hope. This book is full of encouragement. You were placed upon this earth to fulfill a purpose that only you can fulfill. God can, and will, use all that you have been through to accomplish that purpose. Whether or not you feel you have made a mistake, there is always redemption. There is always a way out. There is always a light at the end of a dark tunnel. You were made to live with purpose.

Chapter 4

Created with Purpose

Each of you has a specific destiny to fulfill on this earth. Some of you have more masculine traits and qualities, and others tend to lean toward more feminine characteristics. Each individual is an extraordinary creation, handcrafted by a Father who loves you; by *the* Father who knows everything about you. He dreamed you up before the beginning of time. You are wired to live with purpose, fulfilling the number of days marked out for you on this planet.

It's okay to be a sensitive boy who likes to play with dolls and experiment with his sister's makeup or dresses. It's okay to be a tough girl who dons camouflage and pretends to be a soldier fighting off enemy troops. Each of you is wired differently and each unique characteristic, personality trait, and feature is to be celebrated; not hidden, ridiculed, or made fun of.

Though our feminine and masculine qualities greatly vary from human being to human being, the issue of gender goes back to the beginning of time and is established by God himself. *Genesis 5:2* in the Bible says, *"He created them male and female and blessed them. And he named them 'Mankind' when they were created."* Did you hear that? He BLESSED THEM! God blessed your gender.

There are two genders established by the Creator of the Universe. Who is mankind that we should come along and decide to add to the gender list? It has become completely out of control. It seems that each and every day a new gender is added to the ever growing list of genders. New college courses and majors have been created to accommodate this current epidemic. Gender clinics and hospitals are increasing by the day. When will society stand up and say enough is enough? Depression, anxiety, and suicide rates are on the rise. Children do not know who they are or what they were created for. There is confusion all around.

Bodily mutilation is occurring at an alarming rate as we have stood silent and watched the medical industry destroy the next generation. If you have been a victim of this terrible gender identity confusion revolution, I ask for your forgiveness that I, that we, did not stand up for you. I pledge, in the presence of God, to be here for you now, to wade with you through the disorientation, the anger, the lies, the bitterness, the loneliness, the grief, and the heartache that you have walked through.

War was once waged with swords, guns, and weapons of mass destruction. Today, it takes a more insidious form—fought through the spread of ignorance, division, confusion, and deception, with the aim of capturing the minds of our youth. History offers sobering examples, such as Hitler's regime, which sought to eliminate entire groups of people who did not align with his ideology. That campaign of destruction began not with bullets or bombs, but with the indoctrination of the younger generation.

Unfortunately, children don't get to choose where they land on this planet. I thank God that I was raised in a home that had morals. Right was right and wrong was wrong, based on the plumbline of God's Word, the most popular book in history. This book, the Bible, is without error, no matter how many languages it is translated into. This book is the standard by which God's creation is to live. When we live by this standard, we live in peace and joy. When we don't, there is chaos and turmoil at every turn. When society decides that we are allowed to make up our own set of morals, and that *we* get to determine what is right and what is wrong, evil and the decay of humanity accelerates at an alarming speed. You can see this same pattern emulated throughout history.

* * *

My testimony is this: I was created as a girl, and though I did not like it as a child, I was allowed to live life with purpose. I was permitted to play with the boys, and do "boy" activities, without being encouraged to mutilate my body. Today I am so thankful to be the woman God has created me to be, and that nobody had the influence or the power to change my gender when I was growing up, or to put me on destructive medication and hormones for the rest of my life. God has filled me with purpose and a unique destiny that only I can fulfill. God doesn't make mistakes. I was born with desires. Those desires have matured, and the Lord has transformed me into the person he destined for me to be from the beginning of time. Today I continue to live a beautiful life as a wife to my college sweetheart, as a mother to my children, as a grandmother to my grandchildren, and as a proponent of truth to help shatter the lies that have come in to destroy the next generation.

It's time for the parents and the grandparents to stand up for you, the next generation. You cannot make these huge, life-altering decisions on your own, and it would not even be on your radar if it wasn't being inundated into government, society, the media, and our educational systems.

I'm asking the Lord to forgive us for allowing these evils to infiltrate so quickly as we remained silent, not wanting to offend. It's time that we stand up and stop the madness! We must speak and act before we no longer have the power to speak or to act. It's time that we arise and shine a light on this perverse darkness! I'm calling all parents and grandparents to save the one! You may not have the power to do everything, but you have the power to do something! Ask the Lord: "What is my role? Why am I here at this moment in history?" God wants to use you to make a difference. He is calling you out! It's time to arise and shine!

> Arise, shine, for your light has come, and the glory of the Lord rises upon you. See, darkness covers the earth and thick darkness is over the peoples, but the Lord rises upon you and his glory appears over you. (Isaiah 60:1–2)

To those whom we didn't stand up for, please forgive us. We are here for you now. We are here to walk with you, hand in hand, as you cling to the One True God who will see you through. He has not given up on you. He has not turned his face from you. He is calling you by name. Soften your heart towards him and watch as the miracles unfold. You will feel his tangible presence and his healing love encountering your innermost being. Let him heal you from the inside out and watch your God-given destiny unfold before your very eyes.

What the enemy meant for evil, to destroy you, God is turning around for your good. *"That is what the Scriptures mean when they say, 'No eye has seen, no ear has heard, and no mind has imagined what God has prepared for those who love him'"* (1 Corinthians 2:9, NLT). Let hope rise within your spirit. No matter the season of life you find yourself in, God is preparing to use your journey in profound and unexpected ways to bless and inspire the next generation. You are a destined world changer. Everything you've been through has marked you and brought you to this very moment for a purpose.

Though the enemy may have tried to steal your identity and derail your destiny, the Lord has redeemed you, chosen you, and is preparing to work through you in ways beyond anything you could have imagined. He is not finished with you.

Answer his call. Surrender, and watch as he unfolds a miraculous story through your life—one more fulfilling than you ever dreamed possible. Clarity is breaking forth, and every shadow of confusion is being cast out.

Chapter 5

From Confusion to Clarity

We have all walked in extreme measures of clarity and equal measures of confusion. I'm asking Jesus right now to give every person who is reading these words, a season of clarity over every ounce of confusion and deception that has infiltrated your mind and your heart. Allow Jesus to take immediate authority over your thought process right now and to clothe you with his mind, his truth, and his resurrection power. He is the only one able to do this, because of the authority given to him, through what he accomplished on the cross. If you don't know the story, I encourage you to read the greatest love story ever written for your life in the book of John in the Bible. Ask God to speak to you as you read. He will reveal himself to every longing heart. The Word of God is living and active (*Hebrews 4:12*). His words will penetrate the very depths of your soul. They will usher in transformative power to change you and to pull you from darkness to light, from the power of Satan to the power of God (*Acts 26:18*).

All of us were born with decisions to be made. Each decision builds upon the next. We are born to live in communion with God, our Creator. When we choose this, life is fulfilling and full of peace. Unfortunately, there is an enemy out there who wages war against every part of our lives day and night. He ushers in fear, confusion, anxiety, lack of clarity, lies, deceit, anger, lust, perversion, depression, and all forms of negativity. When we give in to those lies, temptations, and negative emotions, it leads us to actions that are not in our best interest. As we give in to the first little lie, it opens the door to make the next bad decision easier and easier.

THUS ENTERS CONFUSION.

But confusion doesn't have to overtake you! Clarity can rule your heart and your mind. When Jesus died to take on all of the wrongs of the world, he rose in victory. When he resurrected into heaven, he did not leave you alone. He left his Spirit with you. The Holy Spirit is our built in counselor, teacher, friend, and guide. He is the one who brings wisdom and revelation.

You never have to wonder or question whether or not you are making the right decision when you stop to ask the Holy Spirit and let him lead you.

It is his delight to guide you into all truth and to bless your life. Only God can usher in the peace and the joy that will lead you into a life of abundance. You have a choice to make every moment of every day.

When you surrender your life to Jesus, you become a spiritual being living in a physical body. You were dreamed up in the mind of God before the beginning of time. You are his joy. He longs to be in a relationship with you. He is not a far off distant God. He is a personal, loving God who has your best interest always at the forefront of his mind.

You no longer have to live in confusion, anxiety, depression, loneliness, and fear. God is the God of clarity, peace, hope, joy, and unsurpassing love. No matter what you have done or not done, God is waiting for you to call out his name. Stop and get right with him. Do it now! Don't delay! Pray a simple prayer with me:

Dear Father in heaven,

I have felt lost and alone my whole life. I'm asking you for help. I'm ready to surrender to you. Please forgive me for the many ways I have messed up and gone against your desires, plans, and purposes for my life. Thank you for being a kind and loving Father. Thank you for forgiving me, and for providing me an opportunity for a fresh start. Thank you that your mercies are new every morning. I love you and ask you to infiltrate my very being and make me new. I choose to trust you Lord. I give my life back to you.

In Jesus' name I pray, Amen.

The antidote to confusion? Jesus!

His perfect love will get rid of all confusion, usher in clarity of mind, and bring clear solutions to every conflict, decision, and question that you face from now to eternity. In *Jeremiah 33:3*, God urges his children to *"Call to me and I will answer you and tell you great and unsearchable things you do not know."*

Where you have felt hopeless, depressed, anxious, discouraged, confused, and ready to give up, Jesus is the answer. Call upon his name and watch all confusion fade. Peace will infiltrate and you will never have to walk alone again. Let him become your everything. He is standing at the door of your heart, knocking. Open the door and let him in. This will be the best decision you have ever made and it will be life altering. Your life is full of value and purpose in the eyes of God. Let him take you from survival mode to thriving in every way. Do not delay! Don't put off what you can do right now. Surrender.

No matter how far you have strayed from God, he is always waiting with open arms. Even if you have never known God or been exposed to him in any way, he is still there waiting for you! It doesn't even matter if you have already transitioned or changed your gender in any way. Whatever stage you are in, God will use your life in an amazing way if you will permit him. You will be the answer to somebody else's pain. Your life is so important. I can't even begin to tell you how much you matter! You were destined to live on this earth during this exact historical period in time. God has written you into his story line. Listen as he is always speaking to you and revealing to you your unique destiny.

Chapter 6

Messages from God

E very human being was born with a longing, a deep unsatiated desire, to know God. Some people hear his voice. Others feel distant and separated from him. There are seasons of loneliness, grief, and despair; but there are always seasons of deep satisfaction available to you which include love, peace, and joy; where you know who you are and why you were placed on this earth.

You will experience moments in life of being confronted by counterfeit ideologies. These falsities are brought forth through demons who work for Satan, the enemy of your soul. They present themselves as angels of light, but they come to deceive and draw you away from the One True God. They come with temptations and things that are shiny and beautiful, but in reality, the shine will wear off and true torture will take over your spirit, body, and soul if you go down the path where they lead.

How do you differentiate between what is true and what is counterfeit? You must go back to the Word of God. The Bible is the living Word of God. These words of life know exactly how to speak to your heart, your deep longings, and your needs. The Word of God comforts, teaches, trains, equips, and builds you up. It does not tempt you with false power or prestige. It always points to God and it always brings peace and clarity.

The Bible is the number one selling book in all of history, with more than five billion copies sold and distributed worldwide. The content was written over a course of more than 1500 years. People have risked their lives to get ahold of this book. People have given their lives protecting this book. Governments and nations have outlawed this book. This is all the evidence you need to know that this must be a powerful resource! It is the only book that will survive all of eternity. Did you know that God himself said,

> *In the beginning was the Word, and the Word was with God, and the Word was God. He was with God in the beginning. Through him all things were made; without him nothing was made that has been made. In him was life, and that life was the light of all mankind. The light shines in the darkness, and the darkness has not overcome it. (John 1:1–5)*

Wrap your head around that! The Bible, the Word, is God. The Bible is the source of all truth, written before the beginning of time.

How does God speak to us?

He speaks to us in many ways, but the most prevalent way is through his Word. *John 1:14 says, "The Word became flesh and made his dwelling among us. We have seen his glory, the glory of the one and only Son, who came from the Father, full of grace and truth." The Word became flesh* refers to God becoming man and coming to earth to redeem us from our lives of sin and evil. He came to us in the form of his son, Jesus.

While on this earth, Jesus said, *"I am the way, the truth, and the life. No one comes to the Father except through me" (John 14:6).* If Jesus said this, he is either lying, or crazy, or... he is who he says he is. As we study history, nobody ever called Jesus a liar, or a lunatic. Most people who didn't believe he was God still called him a prophet, a teacher, or a good religious leader. But he, himself, said that he is God. If you don't believe him, ask him to reveal himself to you. He will *always* answer that prayer! There are more documented testimonies of Jesus answering that prayer than you will ever be able to digest.

In February of 2024 as the war between Hamas and Israel raged on in the Gaza strip, 200 Muslim men had dreams of Jesus on the same night.[10] All of them came to know him through this miraculous experience. He is waiting for you to call on his name. He is waiting to reveal himself to those of you who are ready for the truth. Don't wait another moment! Call upon the name of Jesus!

To those carrying anger over the harmful advice you received, the misguided guidance, and the adults who failed to protect you in moments of deep vulnerability—please stay with me. I invite you to begin the process of healing. Together, we will confront that anger and navigate the deep, tumultuous emotions that have held you back. There is freedom ahead, and a God-given destiny waiting to unfold in your life.

God can turn your situation around in an instance. Sometimes he walks you through a process because he is the only one who truly knows exactly what you need. He holds your heart in the palm of his hands. Surrender your heart to him and watch your own personal miracle unfold. Give him the anger. Give him your grief. Did you know that he catches every one of your tears in a bottle? *"You keep track of all my sorrows.* **You have collected all my tears in your bottle.** *You have recorded each one in your book"* (Psalm 56:8 NLT).

The Lord of your life has a message that is personal for you. It is specific to your life calling. Sit in his presence and give him permission to love on you and to speak to your heart. This means turning off the external noises from your phone, computers, ipads, tablets, watches, and other technology to sit quietly with him. To some of you this is a foreign concept. Begin with just five minutes a day. Ask him questions and allow time for him to speak to your heart and mind. Keep a journal nearby and record what comes to your mind. Any negative thoughts are from the enemy of your soul, the devil. God always speaks with kindness and love. He knows what you need to hear. He knows everything about you. Sit and listen to what he has to say about you and the direction he would like to lead you in. He is a good, good Father. He will never fail you.

"For God so loved the world that he gave his one and only Son, that whoever believes in him shall not perish but have eternal life."
John 3:16

Chapter 7

What Now?

Some of you reading this book have already transitioned into your desired gender. You may be on hormones and / or medication for the rest of your life. Don't worry! Don't fret! None of this has caught God by surprise and he has an answer for every one of you. One thing I have learned through life is that no matter how many times I mess up, no matter how many times I go down the wrong path, make a mistake, or fail God... He never fails me! He is faithful and has a solution and a remedy for every situation that I have trapped myself in, and for every wrong decision I have made.

Trust me when I say that God is going to use every trial you have walked through for your good. He can redeem even the person who has walked the farthest away. We see many examples of this in the Bible, one in particular regarding a man named Saul who used to torture and kill those who believed in Jesus. Did God condemn him to death? No! Instead he saved him and used his life to write much of the New Testament of the Bible.

That is the redeeming power of God, given to those who receive his free gift of grace. There is no condemnation when we come to Christ Jesus. He removes all guilt and shame and allows us to walk in his redemptive freedom.

Some of you will need to forgive those who gave you bad counsel and helped you to transition into something God never intended for your life. This may include parents, friends, doctors, counselors, teachers, etc. I'm pleading with you to sit in the presence of the Lord and ask him to bring to mind every person you need to forgive. As he brings each one to the forefront of your mind, say out loud, "I forgive (*name*), I bless (*name*), and I release (*name*)". Do this over and over until you feel it! Do this until hearing their name no longer triggers you. Then you will truly know you are walking in forgiveness.

Forgiveness is such a key in your healing process. When you hold onto unforgiveness, it does not hurt anyone but yourself! The person you are not forgiving has most likely gone on with their life, not even considering the damage and pain they have caused you. You are the one being held captive by not forgiving them. When we allow ourselves to walk in anger, bitterness, and unforgiveness, a whole array of health conditions can arise.

I know this first hand. I walked in bitterness and unforgiveness for many years, and as a result I suffered from fibromyalgia, chronic fatigue syndrome, Hashimoto's thyroiditis, Sjogren's syndrome, and migraine headaches for over 20 years. Once I began to understand the connection between my mental, emotional, physical, and spiritual health, my healing journey began. Today I operate in forgiveness, and I continue to bless those who meant me harm. I have moved on and am free from all of the above illnesses and all medications associated with them.

The story of the woman at the well, found in *John 4*, is a powerful testament to the redemptive love and forgiveness of Jesus. Though she had a painful past—having had five husbands and living with a man who wasn't her husband—Jesus spoke to her with compassion, not condemnation. He revealed that he knew everything about her, yet offered her "living water" and the truth that would set her free. His love transformed her shame into purpose. Filled with joy, she ran to tell her community about Jesus, becoming one of the first and most passionate evangelists, boldly sharing the good news of her Savior with everyone she met.

It's time to receive forgiveness from your Father and to forgive all who have hurt you. There are many fathers and mothers in the faith who are available to help you. We are here to help you wade through the questions, the doubts, the fears, the anger, and the unknown. Many of you have grown up without mothers and fathers who were physically and / or emotionally available to you. Some of it was due to poor choices they made, but others were trying their best to just hold on and survive. Life is not easy. We need each other. It's time to forgive your past and move forward with great anticipation into your future that is bright and full of promise. One of my favorite verses in the Bible reminds me to keep my gaze forward, set on Jesus.

Brothers and sisters, I do not consider myself yet to have taken hold of it. But one thing I do: Forgetting what is

*behind and straining toward what is ahead, I press on
toward the goal to win the prize for which God has called
me heavenward in Christ Jesus. (Philippians 3:13–14)*

The enemy tries to get us to look back, slinging condemnation, regret, and shame on us. The only time we should look back is to forgive someone or to ask forgiveness of someone. Other than that, we need to keep our gaze forward to all that God has for us to fulfill on this earth.

As mature believers in the faith, there are mothers and fathers who are here for you. We want to be a voice of truth in your lives. Where there has been confusion, lies, deception, and evil causing you to feel hopeless, depressed, and as if you will never be good enough; we are here to offer hope, direction, prayer, guidance, and a safe place to receive counsel while you work through your specific situation. Refer to the list of organizations and resources at the end of this book. These ministries and websites are full of people with real life stories of being set free and transformed by the grace and blood of Jesus. You may reach out at any time for help through your journey.

We are cheering you on! God has a beautiful plan of restoration for your life. Your future is bright in Jesus. He will not only restore the lost years, the lost dreams, and the lost visions; he will make more of your life than you ever dreamed, hoped, or imagined.

It's time! The Father says, "Come home. I am waiting with open arms."

Pray with me:

Father God,

You are worthy to be praised! Thank you for calling me by name. Forgive me for the years where I did not hear your voice or heed your call. I am sorry Lord. I turn to you now. I give you my life. I ask you for your forgiveness, redemption, and restoration for the years the enemy has stolen from me. I do not want to waste another year or another moment apart from you. Please save me as I call upon your name. Thank you for hearing the cries of my heart and rushing in to wipe away my tears. I am your child. Thank you for creating me uniquely and with purpose. Allow me, by your grace, to fulfill my God-given destiny on this earth. Thank you for your grace and your mercy. I am yours, Lord. Have your way with me.

In Jesus' name I pray, Amen.

Chapter 8

Known and Loved

To those who have felt unseen, unheard, and misunderstood—know this: You are known by God! You are not an accident, nor are you forgotten. Every part of your being, every thought, every tear, and every longing has been held in the hands of a Creator who loves you beyond measure.

You are Fearfully and Wonderfully Made!

Psalm 139:13–14 says, "For you created my inmost being; you knit me together in my mother's womb. I praise you because I am fearfully and wonderfully made; your works are wonderful, I know that full well."

These words are a reminder that God was intentional in creating you. Your struggles, your identity, and your search for peace are not overlooked by him.

In the depths of your questioning, God is not absent. He sees you. He loves you. He understands what it is like to feel deep sorrow and confusion. Jesus himself walked the earth and experienced rejection, suffering, and the weight of human struggle. *Hebrews 4:15* assures us that he is a High Priest who can sympathize with our weaknesses because he was tempted and tested in every way, yet without sin.

A Love That Does Not Fail

There may be times when you have felt rejected—by family, by society, even by the Church. But God's love does not waver based on human opinions. *Romans 8:38–39* declares:

> *For I am convinced that neither death nor life, neither angels nor demons, neither the present nor the future, nor any powers, neither height nor depth, nor anything else in all creation, will be able to separate us from the love of God that is in Christ Jesus our Lord.*

You are loved beyond your human understanding. You are not too far gone, not too broken, and not beyond the reach of God's grace. The world may not always offer you the acceptance you long for, but in Christ, you are fully known and fully loved.

Peace in the Midst of the Storm

Isaiah 26:3 says, "*You will keep in perfect peace those whose minds are steadfast, because they trust in you.*" The search for peace can be overwhelming, but God offers a peace that goes beyond what the world can give. This is not a temporary or shallow peace but a deep assurance that you are held in his hands.

No matter where you are on your journey, know that God is walking with you. He is near to the brokenhearted (*Psalm 34:18*), and he longs to bring healing to the wounded places in your soul. His love is not dependent on how others see you or how you see yourself—it is rooted in who he is.

An Invitation to Walk with Him

Jesus calls us to himself, saying in Matthew 11:28–30,

> *Come to me, all you who are weary and burdened, and I will give you rest. Take my yoke upon you and learn from me, for I am gentle and humble in heart, and you will find rest for your souls. For my yoke is easy and my burden is light.*

This is his invitation to you. You do not have to carry your burdens alone. Whether you are wrestling with questions of identity, faith, or belonging, he invites you to walk with him. He promises to be with you, to give you rest, and to show you a love that never fades. You are not alone. You are deeply known and immeasurably loved. And that truth will never change.

Blessing instead of Cursing

As I mentioned previously, I personally suffered from numerous autoimmune diseases for many years. One day when I was praying for healing, the Lord brought to mind how throughout my life I had cursed my body in wishing I had been born a male. I immediately confessed this to the Lord and asked for his forgiveness. I began to thank him for my body, my female organs, and all that came genetically with being a woman. I began to speak blessings over my God given gender. This was one of the many keys to victory that the Lord gave me throughout my healing journey.

I can honestly say today that I am grateful for the person God created me to be. I would not want it any other way. I'm so thankful that I am a woman, married to my beloved husband. We have been blessed with children and grandchildren to love on. I am a new creation in Christ Jesus. He has redeemed my life from the enemy's plans and filled me with an overflowing faith that no matter what happens, he is always walking with me and will use every circumstance I wade through for his glory and his divine purposes.

This same God who redeemed my life from the plans of the devil is here for you right now. Allow him to do it his way. He can take every wrong you have done and make it right. He can take every wrong done to you and use it for good in your life. Surrender to him now. Trust him. Though the world and everyone in your life may have failed you, he will never fail you.

Chapter 9

Finding Peace in God's Design

I n moments of deep questioning and struggle, when the weight of gender identity confusion or gender dysphoria feels overwhelming, it is essential to seek solace in the unwavering truth of God's love. He created each of you with intentionality, purpose, and an identity rooted in him.

God Knows and Sees You

The journey of understanding oneself can be complex, but it is comforting to remember that God knows you deeply and intimately. *"Before I formed you in the womb I knew you, before you were born I set you apart..." (Jeremiah 1:5).* Your emotions, struggles, and identity are not hidden from him. He walks alongside you, offering his presence, peace, and guidance. In moments when confusion and distress seem unbearable, rest in the knowledge that he is near.

The Call to Trust in Him

Proverbs 3:5–6 encourages us to *"Trust in the Lord with all your heart and lean not on your own understanding; in all your ways submit to him, and he will make your paths straight."* Even when your feelings conflict with what you have known, God invites you to trust in his plan. This does not mean your struggles are invalid or that your pain is unseen, but rather, it affirms that he is present and will lead you through every trial.

A Loving and Compassionate Savior

Jesus Christ, who walked this earth in human form, understands suffering and struggle. He extended love to those who felt outcast, misunderstood, and brokenhearted. *"The Lord is close to the brokenhearted and saves those who are crushed in spirit" (Psalm 34:18).* If you feel weighed down by questions of identity and belonging, Jesus extends his arms to you, offering a love that surpasses all human understanding.

A Secure Identity in Christ

The world often tries to define us by external standards, but God calls us to find our true identity in him. Over the past 10+ years, there has been a significant rise in the number of individuals identifying with and living out an LGBTQ+ lifestyle. Much of this increase stems from confusion about identity—an uncertainty about who they truly are and where their identity is ultimately rooted.

No matter what emotions or struggles you may face, your worth and identity are secure in Christ. He calls you his beloved, his chosen, and the apple of his eye. Your biological sex, gender, or sexual orientation do not ultimately define who you are—God does. He alone is the author of your identity, and it is in him that your true value and purpose are found.

As someone who is heterosexual, I don't identify myself by that label. While it is part of my genetic makeup, it does not define the core of who I am. Yet for many in the LGBTQ+ community, terms like gay, lesbian, or transgender often become central identifiers. You are so much more than your sexual orientation or gender expression. When your identity is firmly rooted in who God created you to be, life opens up with deeper meaning and greater purpose.

Walking in Faith and Community

You are not meant to walk this journey alone. Surround yourself with those who will uplift you, pray for you, and remind you of God's truth. *Ecclesiastes 4:9–10* says, *"Two are better than one... If either of them falls down, one can help the other up."* Seek a trusted Bible believing community where you can express your thoughts and feelings openly, knowing that you are loved and supported.

I have witnessed too many good families torn apart by the lies of gender dysphoria and the embracement of the LGBTQ+ lifestyle. It doesn't have to end this way. Reach out to the parent who has been on their knees weeping and praying for you. Step back into community with true believers who do not sway with the lies of the culture around them. They will help you walk in the power and the truth of Jesus who conquered sin and death. The same resurrection power lives in you! You can overcome all evil that has attempted to overtake you, destroy you, and keep you from eternal life in Jesus.

> *And if the Spirit of him who raised Jesus from the dead is living in you, he who raised Christ from the dead will also give life to your mortal bodies because of his Spirit who lives in you. (Romans 8:11)*

Holding onto Hope

In moments of darkness, hold onto the hope that God is working in your life, even when you cannot see it. *"For I know the plans I have for you,' declares the Lord, 'plans to prosper you and not to harm you, plans to give you hope and a future'"* (*Jeremiah 29:11*). Your story is not over, and God is weaving together a beautiful plan for your life.

As you navigate this journey, lean into his grace. He is faithful, he is loving, and he will never leave you. Rest in his presence, trust in his design, and know that you are deeply cherished.

Chapter 10

Redeemed and Restored

You are not beyond God's grace! Regret is a heavy burden to bear. Perhaps you made choices that felt right at one point, but now you find yourself in a place of doubt, wondering if you can ever be at peace again. If you have transitioned to another gender and now question that decision, you are not alone. God sees your heart, and his grace is sufficient for you. If you are living in a same-sex relationship, God loves you both. He longs for each of you to give your heart fully to him and allow him to become your true love, the One who will never fail you.

God Knows You Completely

Before you were born, God knew you. Remember *Psalm 139:13–14? "For You created my inmost being; You knit me together in my mother's womb. I praise you because I am fearfully and wonderfully made."*

YOU ARE NOT A MISTAKE, and your identity in Christ is more powerful than anything you have done or anything the world tells you that you are.

God does not look at you with condemnation, but with love. He understands the pain, the confusion, and the longing in your heart. You do not have to figure everything out on your own—He is near to the brokenhearted and will guide you on the path of healing.

Jesus Invites You to Rest

Maybe right now, you feel overwhelmed, lost, or ashamed. You do not have to carry this weight alone. Surrender it to him. His love is not conditional on your past decisions—He loves you right where you are and is ready to walk with you toward restoration.

Healing and Moving Forward

If you are struggling with regret, take comfort in knowing that God is a redeemer. *Joel 2:25* says, *"I will restore to you the years that the swarming locust has eaten" (ESV).* No matter what has happened, God can redeem your story. He specializes in bringing beauty from ashes *(Isaiah 61:3).*

Moving forward doesn't have to mean rushing to undo everything—it means allowing God to lead you step by step. Seek his wisdom in prayer, surround yourself with godly counsel, and trust that he will light your path *(Proverbs 3:5–6).*

You Are Loved and Called

Your worth is not determined by your outward appearance, your current gender, your sexual relationships, or your past decisions. It is determined by the love of Christ, who gave his life for you. *Romans 8:38–39* assures us that *"nothing can separate us from the love of God that is in Christ Jesus our Lord."* Not your regrets. Not your doubts. Not even your mistakes.

God still has a purpose for your life. He is not finished with you. Let today be the start of a journey back into his arms, where **true identity**, peace, and restoration are found.

Pray with me:

Heavenly Father,

I come before you with an open heart. I may feel lost and alone, and I don't know what to do, but I know that you see me and love me. Help me to trust in your plan, to find peace in your presence, and to know that my past does not define me—you do. Align me with those who will help me walk out my journey with you in truth. Lead me step by step, and give me the courage to walk in your truth all the days of my life.

In Jesus' name I pray, Amen.

* * *

Today is the first day of the rest of your life. Today marks a new beginning! I rejoice with you, knowing your life has been redeemed for the glory of the Lord! Look up and keep your eyes on Jesus. He will make your path straight and your life beautiful.

Chapter 11

What God Can Do with a Broken, Surrendered Life

There is no mess too great, no failure too final, no story too shattered that God cannot redeem it for his glory. When a life is fully surrendered—broken, bruised, humbled, and laid at his feet—God doesn't just repair it. He transforms it. He turns ashes into beauty, graves into gardens, and shame into testimony. This is the power of a surrendered life in the hands of the Almighty.

Take the addict, for example. I have a dear friend who was lost in the grip of drugs, alcohol, and prescription medication. She was drowning in self-destruction and despair. The world had given up on her, friends had walked away, and even hope seemed to vanish. But God stepped in. My beloved friend, once consumed by addiction, and serving a prison sentence, now walks in freedom—not just for herself, but as a beacon for others. The Lord set her free from her addictions and she now stands in rooms filled with broken people and says, "I was you. But God rescued me." She is now a counselor, mentor, and a living testimony that nothing is too hard for God.

Then there's the story of the man who has spent decades behind bars for murder. His mother travels the world telling his amazing testimony. Society had branded him a murderer, unworthy of a second chance. But inside those prison walls, Jesus found him. Chains fell off that had nothing to do with iron bars. Forgiven, redeemed, and transformed, he began to walk in his new identity in Christ. Now he preaches behind the same bars where he once lived in shame. He leads Bible studies, comforts the hopeless, and speaks life into those the world forgot. His past did not disqualify him—it qualified him to minister to the very ones who need hope the most.

Those walking through gender confusion or identifying within the LGBTQ+ community may not be in a physical prison bound by chains and bars, but many are experiencing a different kind of captivity—a spiritual bondage that hinders them from walking fully in God's purpose for their lives. Yet, there is hope. There is a freedom available that reaches deeper than anything this world offers—a freedom from deception and the weight of sexual brokenness. Many are discovering this truth, stepping away from the lies of the enemy, and embracing their true identity through the redeeming love of Jesus. In him, they are finding healing, purpose, and a genuine sense of belonging.

There are thousands of testimonies I could cite here, but I will tell you of a friend who once lived a life defined by same-sex attraction and the LGBTQ+ lifestyle. With courage and surrender, she chose to walk a different path—not out of condemnation, but out of love for the One who called her to himself. She chooses to live celibate, devoted to Christ, and has found joy in a deep, intimate relationship with Jesus. Though she struggles with something that goes against God's perfect plan for her life, she has chosen not to engage in the sin, but to walk it out in faith and to give her temptations and desires to God. He is using her life powerfully to reach others and pull them out of the pit of destruction. What she has chosen to give up here on earth is reaping great rewards in heaven. She has come to understand that her life is not her own, but is a gift from God.

Some of my other friends who have come out of the LGBTQ+ lifestyle have been delivered of their same sex attraction, and are now married to the opposite sex. They are walking this earth as living testimonies of the transformative power of Jesus Christ. Some have been blessed with children of their own. Their ministries now reach deep into the LGBTQ+ community with compassion, understanding, and truth. They offer a new way of life—not one of rules, but of relationship with Jesus.

These lives remind us that we are not here to collect possessions, chase status, or live for fleeting pleasure. This life is a vapor—a single drop of water in the vast ocean of eternity, a grain of sand on the shores of the beach. What we cling to here, we often lose. But what we surrender to God, we gain multiplied in heaven.

We can't take our houses, our money, or our careers into eternity. The only thing we can bring with us is other people. Souls. Lives touched by the love and truth of Jesus. What we surrender for Christ on earth will be rewarded with glory in eternity. When we give him everything, we discover that we never really lost anything at all.

So if your life feels broken—surrender it. If your past feels too heavy—lay it down. God is not looking for perfect people. He's looking for surrendered ones. And when he finds them, he writes stories that shake the gates of hell and bring heaven to earth.

What part of your story will you give him today?

Chapter 12

God's Plan Conquers the Enemy's Plan

My life has been radically transformed by my God who loves me and has always had my best interest at heart, even when I was making poor choices and rebelling against him. Looking back over the years of my life makes me think of each corner I turned and each decision I made. Some of them drew me closer to the Lord. Other decisions separated me and made me face consequences I could have avoided if I had kept my eyes on Jesus. I am grateful that God's mercies are new every morning (*Lamentations 3:22–23*). Each day we wake up and are given an opportunity for a fresh start, no matter how far off track we may find ourselves.

Upon the writing of this book, I have been married to my beloved, faithful husband for 38 years. I am still deeply in love with him. He is my best friend and soulmate. Together, we raised three beautiful children and are now loving this new season as grandparents. We have walked through moments of great joy and moments of deep sorrow. Because of our commitment to the Lord and to each other, we have weathered each season feeling deeply loved by our Father. We have made many mistakes throughout life, but each one has taught us so much about ourselves, about forgiveness, and about living from God's higher perspective.

You cannot go wrong when you keep your eyes on Jesus and follow his plans for your life. He will always turn you around and set you back on course when you give him permission.

If I do not share the truth with you right here right now I would be failing you in every way. The Lord has saved me from a dark path that the enemy tried to get me to follow, in more than one way, many times throughout my life. But God, in his infinite mercy kept pursuing me, chasing me down, until my eyes were opened and I surrendered to his promise of a better way. I'm so grateful that he never stopped pursuing me. He feels the same way about you! I know you are feeling something stirring in your heart right now. That is the Holy Spirit drawing you to himself. Surrender!

My purpose on this earth is to speak the truth of the One who loves you into your heart—to break the chains of deception, and to reveal the clear contrast between the enemy's destructive plans and the loving plans your Father has for you.

Satan has a plan for your life:

There are only two kingdoms in this world. There is the Kingdom of God and the kingdom of Satan. One brings righteousness, peace, and joy *(Romans 14:17)*. The other breeds destruction and death *(John 10:10)*. Which one will you serve? Which one are you living for?

The enemy of our souls, Satan, has had one main agenda over the decades and that has been the destruction of the family unit. Divorce rates began raging in the 1970's when the "no fault" divorce laws were introduced. By the time my husband and I were raising our children in the 1990's and early 2000's, it was tough to find stable two parent homes. Most of our kids' friends were living in broken homes with single mothers or single fathers doing their best to raise mentally and emotionally healthy children, on their own, while trying to put food on the table. Others lived in blended households, which brought in its own onslaught of problems.

Cohabitation in the United States became common in the late 20th century. And according to the U.S. Census Bureau: By 2005, 4.85 million unmarried couples were living together, and by 2002, about half of all women aged 15 to 44 had lived unmarried with a partner.[11] We have seen the devastating effects of these non-committed relationships involving unwanted pregnancies and abortions, sexually transmitted diseases, a huge influx of young people identifying as homosexual or transgender, and high numbers engaging in polyamory and gender mutilation due to gender identity confusion. This has left an entire generation without the stability that comes from living in a God-ordained family unit.

The destruction of the family unit is not a new thing. The enemy doesn't have a new strategy, only the same old tactics. So what does he do? He uses the same lies over and over again to deceive the next generation, when the previous generation fails to pass down biblical truth, godly wisdom, and divine guidance.

The Bible urges us to pass down the truth of the Lord from generation to generation:

> *My people, hear my teaching; listen to the words of my mouth. I will open my mouth with a parable; I will utter hidden things, things from of old—things we have heard and known, things our ancestors have told us. We will not hide them from their descendants; we will tell the next generation the praiseworthy deeds of the Lord, his power, and the wonders he has done. (Psalm 78:1–4)*

Many of you have not heard the truth passed down from the previous generations. You do not know the teachings of Jesus and his plans for your life. The enemy has taken advantage of this deficit.

There is a true story of destruction documented long ago. There were two cities that flourished in the fertile plain of the Jordan—Sodom and Gomorrah. Rich in abundance but barren in righteousness, they became symbols of unchecked sin and rebellion against the Creator. The cries of their wickedness rose up to heaven, and the Lord, in his justice, came down to see if the outcry was as grievous as it seemed (*Genesis 18:20–21*).

Among their sins, Scripture records that they were proud, arrogant, unrepentant, and given over to sexual immorality (*Ezekiel 16:49–50; Jude 1:7*). Does this sound familiar? When heavenly messengers visited Lot in Sodom, the men of the city surrounded his house, demanding to have sexual relations with them (*Genesis 19:4–5*). This act was not only a grievous violation of hospitality and decency but a manifestation of deep moral corruption.

Because of their unrepentant hearts and persistent sin, God rained down fire and brimstone, utterly destroying both cities (*Genesis 19:24–25*). Their fate stands as a divine warning, not just to one kind of sin, but to all persistent rebellion against God's design for holiness.

Yet even as judgment fell, God's mercy was evident. He delivered Lot and his family—those willing to heed the warning and flee. The message is clear: God's justice is real, but so is his mercy. He calls all people—no matter their background or lifestyle—to repentance and new life through Jesus Christ.

The Bible does not single out one group above others, for *"all have sinned and fall short of the glory of God"* (*Romans 3:23*). Sexual sin—whether heterosexual or homosexual—is serious in God's eyes (*1 Corinthians 6:9–10*). However, it is not beyond his forgiveness. Paul, writing to the Church in Corinth, reminded them that some of them had once lived in such sins—but they were *"washed... sanctified... justified in the name of the Lord Jesus Christ and by the Spirit of our God"* (*1 Corinthians 6:11*).

There is a force at work in this world that seeks to distort and dismantle God's design.

The enemy's plan for romantic relationships is one of confusion, division, and destruction. It manifests in numerous ways such as homosexuality, transgenderism, gender identity confusion, and the embracing of polyamory. Each of these deviations from God's plan leads individuals away from the truth of their identity and purpose.

Homosexuality, in particular, contradicts God's created order for human relationships. In *Romans 1:26–27*, Paul explains that those who reject God's truth fall into dishonorable passions, exchanging the natural use of the body for what is unnatural. The enemy promotes this lie as a viable alternative to God's design, but it only leads to brokenness, unfulfillment, and spiritual emptiness.

Transgenderism and gender identity confusion go hand in hand with this deception, telling individuals that they can choose their identity outside of God's original design. This disregard for the Creator's intentionality in creating men and women in his image causes deep emotional and psychological harm. God's Word teaches that we are wonderfully made, and to deny the gender he has given us is to reject his perfect design (*Psalm 139:14*).

Polyamory, the idea that multiple romantic relationships can coexist simultaneously in a healthy, committed way, is also contrary to God's plan for marriage. In *Matthew 19:5*, Jesus reaffirms the truth that marriage is between one man and one woman, and that this union is intended to be exclusive and lifelong. Polyamory promotes instability, jealousy, and broken trust, which leads to pain and emotional turmoil for all involved. God's design for marriage provides a stable foundation, a refuge of love and mutual support, which is essential for human flourishing.

The danger in embracing the lies of the enemy is not only spiritual; it also ushers in physical and emotional consequences. The consequences of living outside of God's will are evident in broken homes, fractured relationships, emotional distress, and even health risks. God's commandments are not burdensome; they are for our protection and ultimate good. In his wisdom, he has established a way of life that leads to peace, joy, and eternal fulfillment.

The enemy always steals and perverts what belongs to God. One example of this is the LGBTQ+ community adopting the rainbow flag as their symbol of representation. *Genesis 9:12–16* says,

> *And God said, "This is the sign of the covenant I am making between me and you and every living creature with you, a covenant for all generations to come:* **I have set my rainbow in the clouds***, and it will be the sign of the covenant between me and the earth. Whenever I bring clouds over the earth and the rainbow appears in the clouds, I will remember my covenant between me and you and all living creatures of every kind. Never again will the waters become a flood to destroy all life. Whenever the rainbow appears in the clouds, I will see it and remember the everlasting covenant between God and all living creatures of every kind on the earth.*

In the days of Noah, humanity had become deeply corrupt and filled with violence, turning away from God's ways. The

Bible says that God saw the wickedness of mankind and that every thought of their hearts was only evil continually. This grieved God deeply, and he was sorrowful that he had created humans on the earth. In his righteous judgment, God decided to cleanse the earth of its corruption by sending a great flood to destroy all living things. Yet, amid the darkness, Noah found favor in God's eyes because he was a righteous man who walked faithfully with him. After the flood, God made a covenant with Noah and all living creatures, promising never again to destroy the earth with a flood. As a sign of this everlasting promise, God placed a rainbow in the sky—a beautiful reminder of his mercy, faithfulness, and grace. You can read the entire story in the book of *Genesis, chapters 6 - 9* in the Bible.

The rainbow *is not* a celebration of the LGBTQ+ population. **It is an everlasting promise from our Father who loves us**, and is merciful towards us, despite our continual sin and wickedness.

The second example of enemy infiltration in deceiving the LGBTQ+ community is their adoption of the term "PRIDE" to represent their movement. Jesus walked in complete humility, the exact opposite of pride. As I said before, the enemy twists and perverts what God deems as holy.

HERE IS GOD'S PLAN FOR OUR LIVES:

God is holy. He created sex as a beautiful gift within the covenant of marriage between a man and a woman (*Genesis 2:24; Matthew 19:4–6*). Anything outside of that—adultery, fornication, pornography, same-sex relations—distorts his design. But he does not abandon those who are caught in sin. He reaches out in love and truth, calling them to turn, believe, and be made new.

If you are gender confused and / or have embraced the LGBTQ+ lifestyle, if you have never heard the truth, or have walked away from the truth you once knew, know this: **God loves you!** He sees your heart. But he calls you to repent—not because he wants to shame you, but because he wants to set you free. *"If the Son sets you free, you will be free indeed"* (John 8:36).

The story of Sodom and Gomorrah is not just a warning—it's a call. A call to flee from sin, to run to Jesus, and to be part of the Kingdom of God. The ashes of Sodom whisper a truth still relevant today: God's mercy is greater than your past. But his holiness demands a response.

"Today, if you hear his voice, do not harden your hearts."
—Hebrews 3:15

It all goes back to the beginning of time: In the beginning, God created the heavens and the earth, and he created man and woman in his image, distinct yet complementary. In *Genesis 2:24*, we are told, *"Therefore a man shall leave his father and his mother and hold fast to his wife, and they shall become one flesh."* This foundational truth reveals God's divine plan for marriage: a sacred, lifelong covenant between one man and one woman. This covenant is not just a human contract; it is a divine union that mirrors the relationship between Christ and his Church (*Ephesians 5:31–32*).

Marriage, as designed by God, is the cornerstone of human society.

It is intended to reflect his glory, bringing forth children to be raised in the nurture and admonition of the Lord, providing a stable environment for families, and fostering love, unity, and mutual respect. This divine order is not arbitrary; it is rooted in God's wisdom for our flourishing. When we live according to his plan, we experience peace, joy, and fulfillment as we align our lives with his perfect will.

God's plan for marriage between a man and a woman is a reflection of his covenant with his people. It is not outdated or oppressive; it is a beautiful and life-giving structure that promotes love, safety, and the flourishing of humanity.

When we live according to God's design, we experience the abundant life he promises. Anything outside of this design only brings heartache and destruction, as it cuts us off from his perfect will.

Therefore, we must stand firm in God's truth and protect the sanctity of marriage as he established it. Only through covenant marriage—between one man and one woman—can we experience the fullness of God's blessings, peace, and joy. This is the only way that leads to true fulfillment and the well-being of individuals, families, and society as a whole.

Not everyone will marry in this life and that is okay. In the Bible, the Apostle Paul actually commends those who choose to stay single. In *1 Corinthians 7*, Paul gives practical advice regarding marriage and singleness. Paul teaches that because of the present distress (likely persecution or hardship) and the shortness of time (either due to Christ's imminent return or urgency of the mission), it may be better to remain single. Singleness allows a person to focus fully on serving the Lord without distraction, while marriage brings additional worldly concerns, like pleasing a spouse.

- *1 Corinthians 7:26–29*, Paul says, *"Because of the present crisis, I think it is good for a man to remain as he is..."*
- *1 Corinthians 7:32–34*, he explains that unmarried people can devote themselves to the Lord, while married people are concerned with worldly matters and pleasing their spouse.
- *1 Corinthians 7:35*, Paul clarifies that he's not laying a trap, but is offering advice for undivided devotion to the Lord.

Paul acknowledges marriage as good, and even necessary for some, but emphasizes that singleness can be a gift that enables more focus on God, especially in urgent times.

If you are gender confused or struggle with same sex attraction, singleness is a viable, healthy option. The Lord may be calling you to this great assignment where you will be undivided and solely set apart for his purposes.

For those of you who have already gone against God's design for your life, it is never too late to turn your life around. God is the God of redemption, deliverance, and restoration.

I know many people who have had radical, transformative turnarounds when they fully surrendered their lives to Jesus.

He is the only one who will NEVER fail you.

Are you feeling the tug in your heart as you read these words? That is the Lord God wooing you back home. Surrender and watch him turn your life around. He will reinstate your purpose and set you on solid ground. He will align you with a group of like-minded believers, place you in family, and use your life for his glory.

Pray with me:

> *Lord, I'm ready. I don't know how to do it or what it will look like, but I trust you as my good and faithful Father. Please forgive me for the times I have wronged you, both knowingly and unknowingly. I am ready to surrender my life to you. I'm ready to die to my past life of sin and to live free in you. Thank you for sending your Son, Jesus, to die for my sins. Thank you for raising him from the dead so that I am forgiven and set free. I receive this free gift now. Turn me from my selfish ways and evil desires, and make me a new creation, useful to you today and forevermore.*
>
> *In Jesus' mighty name, I pray. Amen.*

A Love Letter from the Father to the Gender Confused

My Beloved Child,

I see you. I see beyond the confusion, the pain, the questions, and the mask you sometimes feel you have to wear. I see the parts of your heart no one else sees. I know the ache you carry—the longing to feel whole, to be known, to belong. I know the thoughts that swirl in your mind, the tension between who you feel you are and who you've been told you should be.

Let Me speak into that space with the voice that formed you from the dust.

You are not a mistake.

You were made by My hands, crafted with purpose, intention, and love. Before your first breath, I called you by name. You are fearfully and wonderfully made—not just your body, but your soul, your spirit, your innermost being. I did not make a mistake when I formed you as male or female. What I created was good. The world is broken and confused, but I am not.

63

You may feel disconnected from your body. You may feel like your identity is shifting or uncertain. But I am your anchor. Your identity is not found in your feelings, your past, or even your own perception—it is found in Me. I am not angry with you. I am not ashamed of you. I'm calling you to come to Me—just as you are, but not to stay there. I want to make you new.

The world will offer you temporary affirmation, but it cannot give you the peace your heart longs for. That peace is only found in surrender to Me. Not in reshaping yourself, but in allowing Me to reshape your heart. Come into the truth of who I say you are. My truth is not cruel—it is the doorway to your freedom.

You do not need to carry the burden of redefining yourself. I already defined you when I made you. I designed you with care, with beauty, with purpose. And though the enemy has tried to twist what I created, he does not get the final word—I do.

My Son, Jesus, died for you. Not because you were too far gone, but because you are that deeply loved. He took your shame, your confusion, and your pain upon Himself. He rose to give you a new life—not built on shifting sand, but on the solid rock of truth and love. Through Him, you can be whole—not in the eyes of the world, but in Mine.

You are not alone. I am with you in every tear, every question, every silent cry. I have not forgotten you. I am not finished with you. I will walk with you every step of the way as you lay down what the world has said, and pick up what I have declared over you from the beginning. You belong to Me. I am a good Father who will never leave you.

Come to Me. Let Me speak life where there has been confusion. Let Me speak truth where there has been deception. Let Me speak love where there has been rejection. You are Mine. And in Me—you are enough.

With everlasting love,

Your Father in Heaven

A Love Letter from the Father to the LGBTQ+

My Precious Child,

I have loved you with an everlasting love. Before you were formed in the womb, I knew you. I knit you together with care and intention. You are not a mistake, and your life is not an accident. You are precious to Me.

You may not fully understand My ways, but I see your heart, your longings, your pain, and your hopes. Nothing about you is hidden from Me. And still—I love you. Not because of what you've done or who you think you need to be, but because you are Mine. I created you in My image, for a purpose far greater than what this world can offer.

My dear child, I must tell you the truth—because love that hides the truth is not love at all. I see you walking down a path that leads away from Me. Like every person born into this world, you are tempted to define your identity by feelings, desires, and the voices around you. But I call you to something higher: I call you to Me.

I did not create you for confusion or for brokenness. I sent My Son, Jesus, not to condemn you, but to save you—to rescue you from the bondage of sin, and to bring you into light, freedom, and truth. No matter how deeply rooted something feels in your life, nothing is too strong for My redeeming love.

Jesus gave His life for you so that you could be made new—so that you would not have to be a slave to sin, no matter what form it takes. The world may tell you that love affirms everything you feel—but My love transforms you into who you were truly created to be. I call you out of darkness, not to shame you, but to heal you.

Come to Me, just as you are—but do not expect to stay the same. I love you too much to leave you in anything that separates you from Me. My grace is sufficient, My power is made perfect in your weakness, and My Spirit will help you walk in newness of life.

I know this will not be easy. The cross never is. But in losing your life for My sake, you will find true life. I have so much more for you than what the world offers. I offer you peace that passes understanding, joy that is unshakable, and a place in My eternal family.

Return to Me, My child. The door is still open. My arms are stretched wide. I am not angry with you—I am calling you home. I'm looking down the road and waiting for you with open arms.

With all My love,

Your Father in Heaven

A Love Letter from the Father to the Family Members

To the parents, siblings, and family members who weep for the return of your loved ones,

I see your heart. I see the tears you've cried in silence, the prayers you've spoken through trembling lips, and the questions that echo in your soul. You love your child, your brother, your sister, your grandchild, your family member—and so do I. My heart for them is greater than even yours could ever be, because I formed them with My own hands. I know every hair on their head. I know their struggles, and I see their pain, even the parts they hide.

You are not alone in your sorrow. I, too, know what it feels like to be rejected and misunderstood by those I love. I sent My Son into the world, and many turned away from Him. But My love does not give up, and neither should yours.

Continue to love them—not with a love that agrees with sin, but with a love that stands firm in truth. Do not exchange My eternal truth for temporary peace. I have called you to be a light in the darkness, not to dim the light in hopes of making others more comfortable. You are not their Savior—I AM. But I have placed you in their life to reflect My light, to intercede, to speak, and to stand.

Do not grow weary. Do not let fear silence your faith. Your stand for righteousness is not hatred—it is hope. When you speak truth gently, when you live it consistently, when you refuse to celebrate what breaks My heart, you are planting seeds that I will water in My time.

Do not despair if they seem far from Me. I specialize in calling prodigals home. I see what you cannot. I am working in ways you do not yet see. Keep praying. Keep loving. Keep believing.

But also—let Me minister to you. I know this journey can be isolating. I know the enemy whispers lies to discourage you. Come to Me for strength. My grace is sufficient. My Spirit will give you discernment, peace, and courage. Trust Me with your child. Trust Me with your family members. Trust Me with the outcome. I am more patient than you, and I do not forsake the work of My hands.

And remember: your faithfulness matters. The way you live, the way you speak, the way you hold to truth even through heartbreak—it bears witness to who I am. You may feel like your efforts are small, but I multiply what is surrendered to Me.

I love your children and family members. I want them to return— not just to your arms, but to Mine. And I love you, too. I see your obedience, even when it costs you dearly. Your sacrifice does not go unnoticed. Blessed are you who mourn, for you shall be comforted (Matthew 5:4). Stand firm. I am with you.

Even now, I am drawing their hearts. In the quiet moments, in the middle of their rebellion, in the depths of their confusion—I am there. My Spirit is not limited by walls, distance, or defiance. I whisper truth in the night, I send reminders of My love through unexpected places, and I never stop pursuing. What feels like delay to you is often the slow, tender work of redemption unfolding beneath the surface. Keep trusting Me—I am faithful to finish what I have started.

With enduring love,

Your Heavenly Father

Conclusion

Next Steps:

Reach out to some of the organizations below for resources and guidance to help you in the next leg of your journey.

Be sure to watch the many video testimonies recorded by those who have been transformed and washed in the blood of Jesus. You will be deeply encouraged!

Restored Hope Network:
  Website: restoredhopenetwork.org

Overview: A network of ministries that offers biblical discipleship and counseling for those dealing with same-sex attraction and gender identity issues. They uphold the historic Christian view of sexuality and gender.

Approach: Emphasizes healing and identity in Christ, while promoting biblical transformation and grace-filled truth.

His Wonderful Works:
Website: hiswonderfulworks.com

Overview: His Wonderful Works is a Christ-centered ministry dedicated to bringing hope, healing, and freedom in areas of family, relationships, and sexuality. They collaborate with individuals, churches, and ministries to address sexual and relational brokenness.

Approach:

- Healing Prayer: Facilitates encounters with Jesus for personal healing and wholeness.
- Biblical Teaching: Provides scriptural insights on gender, sexuality, and healthy relationships.
- Parent Support: Offers lay counseling and support groups for parents of individuals identifying as LGBTQ+.
- Events: Hosts events like the *Rising Stronger Summit* to equip leaders in promoting sexual and relational wholeness.
- Resources: Curates a comprehensive list of books, articles, and referrals to trusted ministries and counselors.

Aim to Love:
Website: aimtolove.com

Overview: AIM TO LOVE Ministries focuses on outreach, discipleship, and launching individuals into their God-given purposes. The ministry emphasizes a deep, personal relationship with Jesus and living out one's faith authentically.

Approach:

- Discipleship: Guides individuals in understanding their identity in Christ and walking in their calling.
- Resources: Offers teachings and materials aimed at deepening one's faith and commitment to Jesus.
- Personal Engagement: Provides opportunities to connect directly with the leaders for guidance and support

Focus on the Family:
  Website: focusonthefamily.com

Overview: Focus on the Family offers extensive resources and referrals for individuals and families dealing with gender identity issues. Their approach is grounded in biblical values.

Approach: Compassionate and family-oriented, often emphasizing dialogue, prayer, and support.

Also by Debbie Bilek

Smiling on the Outside, Dying on the Inside

Strategies From Heaven; Contending for the Impossible

12 Strategies From Heaven for the Ekklesia

Parents of Prodigals; 10 Day Strategic Devotional

Becoming Atmosphere Shifters and Destiny Changers

Notes

CHAPTER 1

1   National Health Service (NHS). *Gender Dysphoria*. Last modified November 10, 2022. https://www.nhs.uk/conditions/gender-dysphoria/.

CHAPTER 2

2   Mount Sinai. *Gender Dysphoria*. New York: Mount Sinai Health System. Accessed [October 2024]. https://www.mountsinai.org/health-library/diseases-conditions/gender-dysphoria.

3   CNN. "Study Shows Gender-Affirming Surgeries Nearly Tripled in the US from 2016 to 2019." Accessed [October 2024]. https://www.cnn.com/.

4   National Library of Medicine. "Study Finds Fivefold Increase in Gender-Affirming Procedures from 2016 to 2021." Accessed [November 2024]. https://www.nlm.nih.gov/.

5   Reuters. "While the number of gender clinics treating children in the United States has grown from zero to more than 100 in the past 15 years…" *Reuters*, October 2022. https://www.reuters.com/.

6   LexisNexis Risk Solutions. "Data Shows 133% Rise in Insurance Claims for Gender Identity Care Among U.S. Minors Between 2019 and 2023." Accessed [March 2025]. https://risk.lexisnexis.com/.

7   Michael Searles, "Child under 5 among thousands on gender clinic waiting lists," *The Telegraph*, August 6, 2024, https://www.telegraph.co.uk/news/2024/08/06/child-under-5-among-thousands-nhs-gender-care/.

8   Wikipedia, s.v. "Identity (social science)".

CHAPTER 3

9   National Institute of Mental Health. *The Teen Brain: Still Under Construction*. Accessed [April 2025]. https://www.nimh.nih.gov/health/publications/the-teen-brain-still-under-construction.

CHAPTER 6

10   Michael Foust, "200 Muslims in Gaza Reportedly Accept Christ After Seeing Visions of Jesus in Their Dreams," *Crosswalk*, February 2024, https://www.crosswalk.com/headlines/contributors/michael-foust/200-muslims-gaza-reportedly-accept-christ-seeing-visions-dreams.html.

CHAPTER 12

11   https://en.wikipedia.org/wiki/Cohabitation_in_the_United_States

About the Author

Debbie Bilek is an ordained minister, teacher, author, mentor, and leader with a passion for guiding others toward healing, freedom, and identity. After experiencing her own powerful transformation—physically, emotionally, and spiritually—Debbie now equips individuals and communities to live from a place of truth and restoration. She addresses topics such as emotional healing, identity struggles, spiritual growth, and cultural challenges with compassion, clarity, and boldness. Known for her authenticity and encouragement, Debbie brings practical wisdom and deep insight to every audience.

Debbie is married to her college sweetheart, Bill. She is a devoted mother and grandmother, and is deeply passionate about equipping and empowering individuals across generations to fulfill their God-given purpose.

You can connect with me on:
- https://www.strategiesfromheaven.com
- https://www.facebook.com/strategiesfromheaven
- https://www.youtube.com/@strategiesfromheaven